ICE HOCKEY LEGENDS

Martin Brodeur

Sergei Fedorov

Peter Forsberg

Wayne Gretzky

Dominik Hasek

Brett Hull

Jaromir Jagr

Paul Kariya

John LeClair

Mario Lemieux

Eric Lindros

Mark Messier

CHELSEA HOUSE PUBLISHERS

ICE HOCKEY LEGENDS

ERIC LINDROS

John Kreiser

CHELSEA HOUSE PUBLISHERS
Philadelphia

Produced by Daniel Bial and Associates
New York, New York

Picture research by Alan Gottlieb
Cover illustration by Earl Parker

The Chelsea House World Wide Website address is
http://www.chelseahouse.com

3 5 7 9 8 6 4 2

Library of Congress Cataloging-in-Publication Data

Kreiser, John.
    Eric Lindros / by John Kreiser.
        p. cm.—(Ice hockey legends)
    Includes bibliographical references (p.) and index.
    Summary: A close-up look at the rising hockey star who plays for the
Philadelphia Flyers.
        ISBN 0-7910-4557-9
        1. Lindros, Eric—Juvenile literature. 2. Hockey players—Canada—
Biography—Juvenile literature. 3. Philadelphia Flyers (Hockey team)—
Juvenile literature. [1. Lindros, Eric. 2. Hockey players.] I. Title. II. Series.
GV848.5.L56K74 1997
796.962'092—dc21   97-27361
[B]   CIP
                                                                         AC

CONTENTS

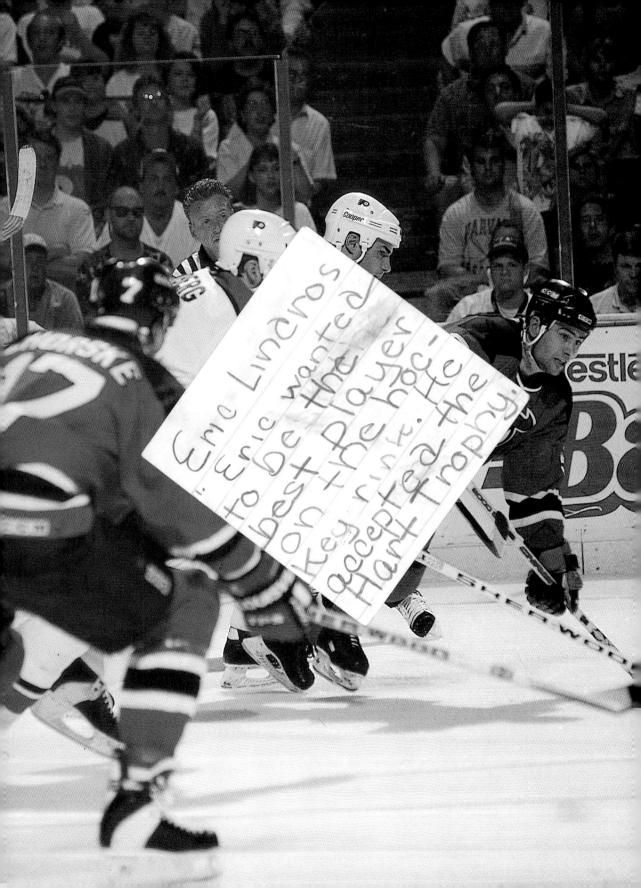

TO BE THE BEST

Eric Lindros grew up wanting to be the best—not just good, not just great, but the best. Now, his efforts were finally being recognized.

In his third NHL season, at the age of 22, there was no doubt that Lindros was already a superstar. If there had been any uncertainty left, all Eric had to do was look up at the screen in the packed room just outside the Hockey Hall of Fame in Toronto. There, for everyone to see, was Lindros skating, Lindros shooting, Lindros hitting, Lindros scoring, Lindros stealing the puck from his boyhood idol—Mark Messier— and setting up goals for teammates.

"It's kind of a fantasy world," he said. "When I was 16, I never thought this kind of thing would ever happen. It's a blur."

It's not as though Eric had never seen highlights of himself—he'd been on highlight films throughout North America since his days in

Wherever Eric Lindros went during the 1995 playoff series against the New Jersey Devils, a defenseman or two was assigned to try to keep him from scoring.

junior hockey. But he had never done it while being proclaimed as the sport's top performer as selected by the men he played with and against.

On that July day in 1995, Eric Lindros received the Lester B. Pearson Award, honoring him as the league's best player as selected by his peers. That night, he also picked up the Hart Trophy, the NHL's own Most Valuable Player trophy.

Much had been expected of Eric Lindros. At 6′5″ and 235 pounds, he was big enough to intimidate opposing players with his physical style of play. But he wasn't just another goon; Eric had speed, passing skills, and a scoring touch almost never seen in players his size.

High expectations had been a fact of Eric's life for years. "They're never going to end," he said. "That's all part of it. But I can't reiterate how important it is to win a Stanley Cup. That's where it's at."

Lindros was the youngest player to win the Hart Trophy since Wayne Gretzky captured it as a 19-year-old in 1980. Eric was so overwhelmed that he had to fight back tears during his acceptance speech. "It wasn't the smoothest ride, but it was one I had to take," he said of his success after the decisions to reject the draft systems at two previous crossroads in his career. "Now, I'm thankful I did."

The Pearson Trophy was special to him because it came from the players he battled regularly. "Receiving the award is a great achievement because it's being given to me by the people I compete with and against on a daily basis," he said in accepting the trophy. "When I recognize those who've received the award ahead of me, I'm in a state of awe. This award is special because it comes from my peers."

Mike Gartner, the president of the NHL Players Association and Lindros's roommate during the 1991 Canada Cup tournament, said that Eric "has developed into one of the premier players in the NHL. This year, he was recognized by his peers as *the* premier player." Lindros knew that he and his team had only scratched the surface of their abilities.

"If you start believing along those lines," he said of comparisons with veteran NHL stars such as Messier, Gretzky, and Mario Lemieux, "you might become satisfied. I certainly don't want to become satisfied with what I've done. I've got a lot of improving to do."

A player's third NHL season is often the crossroads of a career. It's the season in which being a young player is no longer an excuse for lack of production.

Eric was no exception. Though he was acclaimed as a superstar before he ever played a

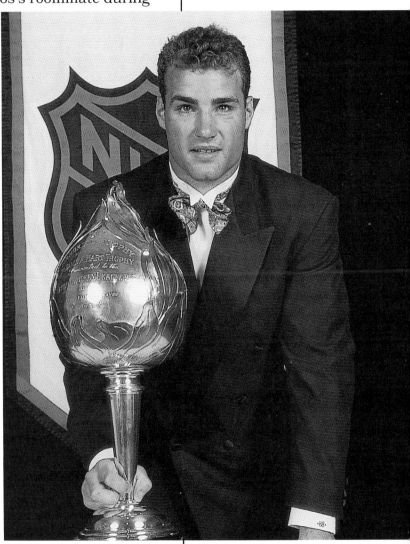

Lindros accepting the Hart Trophy at a ceremony in 1995.

NHL game, his first two seasons were good but not great—and were marked by an assortment of injuries that held back his development. His third season was shortened by 36 games due to the owners' lockout that cut the schedule to 48 games.

However, after a slow start, Philadelphia general manager Bob Clarke traded high-scoring forward Mark Recchi to Montreal for a solid defenseman, Eric Desjardins, and a big left wing, John LeClair, who had never lived up to his potential with the Canadiens.

Coach Terry Murray put LeClair together with Lindros and right wing Mikael Renberg, a sharp-shooter from Sweden who had scored 38 goals as a rookie. The line clicked—and so did the Flyers. Despite their slow start, the team rocketed to the top of the Atlantic Division standings with the play of Lindros and his linemates. Dubbed the "Legion of Doom," they formed the most devastating line in the NHL, presenting a combination of size and skill that proved to be almost impossible for other teams to defend against.

Suddenly, the same people who had been saying that Lindros had a long way to go as a player were talking about his arrival as a superstar. The goals and assists for Lindros and his linemates piled up, as did the victories for the Flyers. Philadelphia, which had missed the playoffs for five straight seasons, not only made postseason play, it finished first in the Atlantic Division.

There were many reasons for the Flyers' success, but they all started with Lindros. He centered the team's number one line, was the top scorer, killed penalties, played on the power play, and usually set the game's tone with a thunderous hit or two.

"Eric Lindros right now is the best hockey player in the world," said Montreal coach Jacques Demers, who had too good a view of "the Great 88" in games like an 8-4 rout of the Canadiens on March 20, 1995, when Eric scored three times. "Lindros will lead the league in scoring for the next seven or eight years."

He did so for the first time in 1994-95, sharing the scoring title with Pittsburgh's Jaromir Jagr. Both finished with 70 points, but Jagr got the Art Ross Trophy, given to the NHL's top scorer, because he had more goals. Had Eric been luckier—or greedier—he might have won the title outright. But an eye injury suffered in the final week of the season against the Rangers knocked him out of the game, and with the playoffs coming up, he sat out the Flyers' last game as well, giving Jagr a chance to catch him.

More important to Lindros, the Flyers were starting to come together as a team. A club that had been lacking a direction and an identity now had one. They were Eric Lindros' team.

"It's starting to come," Eric said. "It's starting to happen now. Pride in Philadelphia is something everyone talks about and thinks about all the time. We're starting to gain some of that back."

NOT JUST A BIG KID

It's not surprising Eric Lindros turned out to be a top-notch athlete. His father, Carl, was drafted by pro hockey and football teams, while his mother Bonnie's sister, Marsha, was a British Commonwealth record-holder in the shotput.

Eric was born on February 28, 1973, in London, Ontario, a small city not far from Toronto, Canada's largest city. Eric was sitting up by June, walking by October, and skating by the time he was 18 months old. Even as a little boy, he was full of energy—a runner, a climber, and a star in the neighborhood games. To drain off some of that extra energy, Bonnie and Carl entered Eric in a little neighborhood hockey league. But he quickly outgrew that and entered the more formal structure of Canadian junior hockey, a path that eventually would lead him to fame in the National Hockey League.

The Oshawa Generals traded away a lot to get Eric Lindros—but he was worth it. In two short seasons with Oshawa, Lindros led the team to a championship.

Though Bonnie wasn't a big hockey fan, it didn't take her long to realize that her son was going to be a special athlete. "I woke up in the middle of the night at a tournament and realized that Eric was just a lot better than the other kids," she said. "He just played smarter hockey. For example, he wouldn't go to where the puck was. He would go where the puck was going to be."

Carl Lindros filled in the in-ground swimming pool to make a backyard rink each winter. From the time he was nine until he was 16, Eric spent an average of two hours a night on the backyard rink, and still found time to skate at home even as his hockey career took off.

Eric was that rare combination: a big, skilled kid who know how to use both his size and skills at a very young age. He raced through the various levels of youth hockey, piling up goals and attracting a lot of attention from NHL scouts, who loved not only his skating, passing, and scoring skills but also his size and his willingness to use it.

Playing for St. Michael's in Junior B hockey, one level below the top level of youth hockey in North America, Eric recorded 67 points in just 37 games—meaning he averaged nearly two points in each game he played. He might have had more, but Eric also rang up 193 minutes in penalties—almost five minutes per game.

NHL scouts could hardly wait for Eric to grow old enough to enter their league. Bob Clarke, a Hall of Fame player for Philadelphia in the 1970s and 1980s (and eventually Eric's boss with the Flyers) said that Lindros was ready to play in the NHL at age 16, two years before he was even eligible to be drafted.

By the start of the 1989-90 season, Eric was 16, and he had dominated midget hockey and was ready to advance to the Ontario Hockey League, one of North America's three Major Junior leagues that provide most of the players who ultimately enter the NHL. Like NHL teams, junior clubs drafted players from the next-highest level, with players having no say about which team selected them.

This was a problem for Carl and Bonnie Lindros. Though hockey was important, they wanted Eric to play near home so that his schoolwork wouldn't be completely disrupted by the additional strain of living far away from home. The Lindroses wanted Eric to play for the Oshawa Generals, a team located in a suburb of Toronto. The Generals boasted a long list of players who went on to star in the NHL, including Bobby Orr, probably the greatest defenseman in hockey history. However, the system under which junior hockey was run gave Eric and his family no choice about where he would be allowed to play.

Instead of Oshawa, Lindros was picked by Sault Ste. Marie, known as "the Soo," a team located hundreds of miles from his home. Carl and Bonnie Lindros were upset, and they sought a way to keep Eric from playing so far away.

"I had a meeting with the people from 'the Soo'

A defenseman tries to hook Lindros at the Ontario Hockey League All-Star Game.

and I told them I wouldn't play for their club," Eric said. "They went ahead and drafted me anyway. I told them I wouldn't show up, and I didn't."

In the tight-knit, orderly world of hockey, a young player who refused to play where he was told wasn't looked upon fondly. Eric, who already was becoming well-known in hockey circles, was regarded by many executives, media members, and fans as a spoiled brat, while Carl and Bonnie were called pushy parents who refused to play along with the system.

Eric and his family stuck to their guns. "Our stand had nothing to do with hockey," said Bonnie Lindros. "It had to do with our lifestyle and our goals for Eric."

Instead of having him play for Sault Ste. Marie, Eric's family boarded him with a family in Farmington, Michigan. He played in a lower-level junior league, which he dominated, scoring 52 points in just 14 games. He also graduated early from Farmington High School.

The Ontario Hockey League saw that Eric and his parents were serious about having Eric play near his home. The league changed the rule that barred trading draft picks, and on December 18, 1989, Oshawa dealt four players and two draft picks plus $80,000 to Sault Ste. Marie for the rights to the most heralded young hockey player since Mario Lemieux.

Despite the high price that Oshawa paid for Eric, the deal quickly proved to be a bargain. Though he played only 25 regular-season games for the Generals, Eric scored 17 goals and added 19 assists for 36 points. He added another 36 points (18 goals and 18 assists) in 16 Ontario Hockey League playoff games, then contributed nine assists in four games as the

Generals won the Memorial Cup, the junior leagues' version of the Stanley Cup, for the first time in 46 years.

Eric kept piling up the points in 1990-91. He won the Ontario League scoring championship with an incredible 149 points in just 57 games. He missed a chunk of Oshawa's schedule during the holiday season to play for Canada at the World Junior Hockey Championships, where he had 6 goals and 11 assists for 17 points—in just seven games. The only sour note to the season was that despite Eric's 38 points in 16 playoff games, the Generals did not qualify to defend their Memorial Cup title.

By now, NHL teams were falling all over themselves trying to find a way to get Eric in the spring of 1991, when he would become eligible for the Entry Draft. The Toronto Maple Leafs, the club nearest to Eric's home, would have loved to have him. But the Maple Leafs didn't have a first-round draft pick.

The last-place finishers turned out to be the Quebec Nordiques, and that won them the right to pick first in the draft. The Nordiques, one of four teams that entered the NHL from the World Hockey Association in 1979, had fallen on hard times in the late 1980s. This was their third straight last-place finish, but they were starting to feel optimistic. Having put together a young team featuring top draft picks Mats Sundin and Owen Nolan, they were now expecting to land Eric Lindros.

There was only one problem: Eric wanted no part of playing in Quebec.

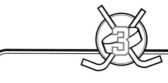

ANYWHERE BUT QUEBEC

The question as the days before the National Hockey League's 1991 Entry Draft in Buffalo, New York, dwindled down was not whether Eric would be the first player picked. At 6'5" and about 225 pounds, Eric towered over the field, literally and figuratively. No, the question was which team would get the chance to make him the richest rookie in hockey history.

Nordiques general manager Pierre Page was besieged with offers, especially after Eric and his family said they weren't interested in playing in Quebec, a small, mostly French-speaking, hockey-mad city about 160 miles from Montreal. The Nordiques had played second-fiddle to the mighty Canadiens ever since they joined the NHL in 1979 after the World Hockey Association broke up, and they looked at Eric as the player around whom they could build their franchise.

Lindros was pleased to be the number one pick in the 1991 draft—but he knew he did not want to play for the Quebec Nordiques.

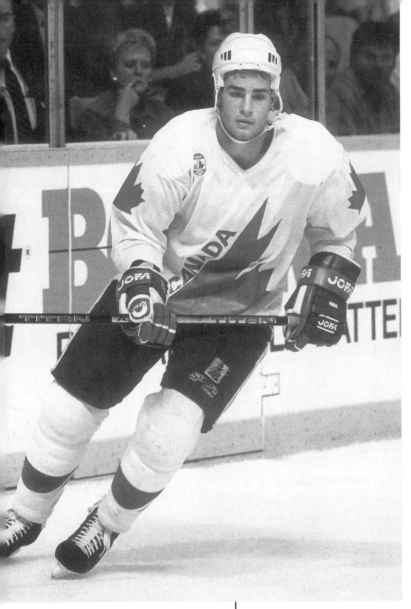

While waiting for his pro status to be worked out, Lindros played on the 1991 Canada Cup team.

But the Lindros family wasn't interested in having Eric play in Quebec. They wanted the Nordiques to trade the pick to enable Eric to play in a bigger city and for a better team.

Page finally called a halt to the circus-like atmosphere three days before the draft when he said the Nordiques would refuse all trade offers and take Eric with the number one pick. "We intend to draft him and then sit down and negotiate," Page said. "Our fans have been very faithful and they deserve something now. We've got to find a way. We've got to use our imagination."

As a hockey player, Page said, Eric was everything a general manager could want. "He's a skilled, physical player, and we're all trying to find those," the Quebec GM said. "Usually, you get a skilled guy and he's not physical, or you get a physical guy and he's not very skilled, or you get a guy who had both but doesn't have character. Put them all together and you've got Lindros. That's why we can't afford to make a mistake."

Eric didn't say much as the big day approached, leaving much of the talking to his agent, Rick Curran, and his mother. Neither was happy about the thought of Eric being picked by a small Canadian city for a team that had finished last in the 21-team NHL for three straight seasons. There was also the language factor: Quebec was the only NHL city in which the public address announcements were made only in French. Many English-speaking NHL players felt uncomfortable living in a city where French was the main (and sometimes only) language spoken.

Many Quebec residents took Lindros's unwillingness to play for the Nordiques as a French-English issue, a sensitive topic in Canada, where many residents of the province of Quebec have campaigned for independence from the rest of the country. Eric and his family said language wasn't the issue.

Regardless, when Page strode to the podium at Buffalo's Memorial Auditorium to announce the first pick in the draft, he didn't hesitate before calling Eric's name. As the applause rained down, Eric strode to the stage to shake hands with Page and Nordiques officials.

To show that he was sincere about not wanting to play in Quebec, Eric followed through on a promise and broke with tradition by refusing to put on a Nordique jersey. As the photographers snapped away, Eric stood with the blue-and-white Quebec jersey slung on his arm.

Eric said the decision not to put on the jersey was simply a matter of not wanting to send out the wrong signal to anyone. "Putting on a jersey would be a commitment," he said. "It would not be right to commit to something I hadn't thought out."

Nordiques officials said that Eric's decision not to wear their jersey didn't matter. "Eric is going to wear the sweater when it counts," team owner Marcel Aubut said. Page, too, told the world that he was sure that Eric would be a Nordique after all was said and done.

"I thrive on situations where people don't believe you can do things," Page said. "We've done it in the past and we'll do it again."

However, playing for the Nordiques was not Eric's only option. At 18, he could still play for the Generals for another two seasons, then re-enter the draft in 1993. A proposed new hockey league, the Continental Hockey Association, was said to be willing to offer as much as $2 million per year for three years to bring instant credibility to their fledgling organization. He could also opt to play for Canada's national team, which would make him part of the Olympic squad that would play in Albertville, France, in February 1992.

"Money is important," Eric said. "But it's not everything. I want to be happy."

One thing that did anger him were accusations that he felt he was more important than the game. "I don't think I'm bigger than the game," he said. "I'm just not going to follow the regular footsteps. It's more than money. It's happiness."

Although talks between Curran and the Nordiques went nowhere, Eric was headed for a training camp in late summer. He was the only non-NHL player invited to play on Canada's entry in the Canada Cup tournament, the unofficial world championship of hockey. Although some fans and writers thought that inviting an 18-year-old to camp was little more than a publicity stunt, Eric wasted no time in showing that he was determined to earn a spot on the team.

Lindros shakes hands with future New York Ranger Alexei Kovalev at the World Junior Championship tournament.

He did the same thing in Team Canada's practices that he had done with the Generals—use his big frame to push his way to the net to create scoring chances, as well as dishing out big hits with regularity. Of course, he took a few hits, too—including one from New York Islanders center Brent Sutter that left him with a mild concussion.

The NHL stars who saw him were impressed. "He's got all the talent in the world and can hold his own anywhere," said Steve Larmer, a star

Canada had to settle for the silver medal in hockey at the 1992 Olympics. Lindros (left) along with Kent Manderville (center) and Gordon Ross Hynes watch the Unified Team (the former Soviet Union) receive their gold medals.

right wing with the Chicago Blackhawks. "He has a natural ability to see things develop on the ice. It's unusual for a man that big to have that much speed and such great hands."

Of course, the issue of where he would begin his NHL career wouldn't go away. *Le Soleil*, a newspaper in Quebec City, claimed that Curran had asked the Nordiques for $3 million per season to sign a contract.

Eric said he was upset that dollar figures discussed at the meeting turned up in the newspapers.

"I think it sort of upset me that there's so much said about many things I've never said anything about," he said of the talks. "A meeting was held and it was supposed to be confidential. A number came out of the meeting. I can't say whether it was too high or too low. How can I comment about things that we agreed we wouldn't talk about?"

On the ice, Eric let his play do his talking. Not only did he make Canada's roster for the star-studded tournament, but he also played a regular shift as the Canadians retained their title. His play was so good that he drew cheers from a crowd in Montreal, the biggest city in the province of Quebec, while leading Canada to a 9-1 victory in a pretournament game. Although he was booed when he took the ice at the Quebec Colisee on September 9 for a game against the Soviet Union, the booing was more of disappointment than anger.

Prior to the game, Eric said that his desire to play somewhere else had nothing to do with Quebec's French culture. "I have nothing against the city of Quebec, nothing against the French people and nothing against the Nordiques," he said. "But I believe I should be able to decide where I want to spend my career."

That place wasn't Quebec.

This kind of thinking was virtually unprecedented in the National Hockey League, where generations of players had played where team owners had told them to play. So instead of heading to his first NHL training camp, Eric returned to the Generals.

"It's a little bit of a letdown," he admitted after reporting to Oshawa on September 22. "But there are things I can still work on. Frustrations are things you can hold within you when you know that at the end of the road, you can work it out."

Eric had an assist in his first game back, a 4-2 victory over Peterborough, but admitted that his play was "horrible."

As a precaution, Eric and his family had taken out a $5 million insurance policy before he returned to the juniors. He had been back only a week when he missed two games after being elbowed during a game, then sat out a three-game suspension for receiving a match penalty.

He wasn't spending all of his time in Oshawa. Eric was dividing his time between the Generals and the Canadian Olympic team, which had "borrowed" him from Oshawa—and he was still answering questions about his NHL future.

"I've got nothing against Quebec. I just don't want to play for the Nordiques or Quebec City," he said in December. "I'd love to play in Montreal. And New York would be a great place to play."

Before the Olympics, Eric made another detour—to Fussen, Germany, for the World Junior Championships. Although he had two goals and six assists in seven games, both Eric and Canada had bad tournaments. The Canadians, accustomed to winning the gold medal at the junior championships, finished below .500 at 2-3-2, ending with three straight losses. Eric was booed constantly and was slowed by the effects of a virus that drained the strength that he relied upon to dominate opponents.

All that the poor showing in Germany did was make Eric more eager to play well in the Olympics. He didn't disappoint, finishing the round-robin portion of the tournament with 4 goals and 6 assists for 10 points, second in the scoring race to teammate Joe Juneau.

Eric had his biggest Olympic moment in the quarterfinal game. With Canada tied with Germany at 2-2 after regulation time and an overtime period, the two teams went to a penalty-shot shoot-out to decide the game. The winner would advance to the semifinals, while the loser would go home without a medal.

Eric was Canada's first shooter and didn't score. After two of the five shooters on each team had scored in the first round, Eric got a chance to redeem himself—and he didn't miss. Goaltender Sean Burke then stopped the German shooter, and Canada advanced to the semifinals—thanks to Eric's goal.

The Canadians downed Czechoslovakia 4-2 to make the finals but were unable to beat the Unified Team, the new name for the old Soviet Union squad. Regardless of the name, the result was a 3-1 loss that sent Canada home with a silver medal.

Eric went back to Oshawa but was injured in the final game of the season, suffering a 25-stitch cut when he was cross-checked in the face. He didn't skate in the playoffs, as the Generals were eliminated in the first round. In all, he wound up playing just 13 games for Oshawa, but managed 31 points, giving him 97 goals and 216 points in only 95 games as a junior.

Now it was time for the NHL.

A FLYER OR
A RANGER?

As the hockey world headed for the 1992 Entry Draft in Montreal, there was more interest in where Eric would be playing that fall than in the players who were about to be picked. Aubut and Page fielded phone calls day and night from teams anxious to take Eric off their hands.

The front-runner seemed to change almost hourly. One writer who flew to Montreal the day before the draft bought three newspapers, each touting a different team said to be close to a deal. By the time he walked into draft headquarters late in the afternoon, none of those teams was now regarded as the likeliest team to make a deal.

The most persistent would-be traders were the Philadelphia Flyers. With a new arena already on the drawing board, the Flyers had seats and luxury boxes to fill, as well as a last-place team that was desperate for a franchise player.

Lindros, now a Philadelphia Flyer, celebrates his first goal as a professional hockey player.

The New York Rangers, a fierce rival of the Flyers, also wanted Lindros, whom they viewed as the potential successor to superstar center Mark Messier. The two had played together at the Canada Cup tournament, and Lindros was eager to learn from "Mess," who had five Stanley Cup rings to his credit from his days with the Edmonton Oilers.

The Flyers were sure they had a deal—especially when Aubut provided them with the Lindros family's home phone number on June 20, the day of the draft. The Nordiques didn't see it that way. Flyers officials were getting ready to celebrate when Aubut called and told them the deal was off, that he had a written agreement for a deal with the Rangers.

Flyers president Jay Snider filed a protest, and NHL president Gil Stein decided to have an arbitrator, Larry Bertuzzi, handle the decision. After five days of testimony by the teams involved and another few days to sort out what had happened, Bertuzzi ruled on June 30 that the trade with the Flyers was the valid deal, even though nothing official had been filed with the league.

Eric was thrilled to know finally where he was going to play. "It's been a long 15 months," he said. "My bags are packed and it feels great. I'm happy I'm going to Philadelphia."

To get Eric's rights, the Flyers gave up five players: starting goaltender Ron Hextall, young centers Peter Forsberg and Mike Ricci, and defensemen Steve Duchesne and Kerry Huffman. They also ceded two first-round draft picks, another player to be named later—and $15 million. No other player had cost as much—not even Wayne Gretzky when he was sent from Edmonton to Los Angeles three years earlier.

Lindros (88), Mark Recchi (8), and Brent Fedyk (18) formed a line known as the "Crazy Eights."

Russ Farwell, the Flyers' general manager, had no qualms about giving up nearly half a team for a player who had yet to step onto an NHL rink. "We drew a line going into the negotiations," Farwell said. "It's been proved lately that a dominant player is the key to a successful year."

Unlike the dragged-out talks with Quebec, Eric, his family, and Curran needed only a couple of weeks to work out the biggest contract ever given to a rookie: a six-year deal estimated to be worth about $21 million. That was an average of more than $3.5 million—more money than any player except Gretzky made.

"It's a relief for me and my family," Eric said after the deal was done. "The whole year was tough on me and on my parents. They tried to

Lindros proudly holds the pucks he used to score his first hat trick.

act as shields and take the hits. For them to stay tough and stand by me was a great asset."

Big salaries mean big expectations from fans. After all, it's their money that goes to pay the players. So Eric tried to convince eager Philadelphia fans that he wasn't Gretzky, Mario Lemieux, and Messier rolled into one.

His biggest asset, he felt, might be his burning need to succeed. "I think it's the desire to win," he said when asked about the strongest part of his game. "I don't shoot like Brett Hull or skate like Paul Coffey. But if you think you can, you're going to get close. They don't ask how pretty the points are, just how many."

Flyers fans couldn't wait to see Eric in a Flyer uniform, or even to buy a Flyer jersey with his name and number—88. One store reportedly sold 550 Lindros jerseys in the month after the trade became official; a store official said the previous high for the month was about 50. Although Flyer jerseys usually sold for $92, Eric's number became a selling gimmick when stores sold the orange, black, and white sweaters for $88.88.

Eric was rested and ready when he reported to his first NHL training camp. The Flyers had decided months earlier to train on Prince Edward Island, a small Eastern Canadian province, and fans flocked to the tiny arena to see the player touted as hockey's next superstar. Eric admitted that he was nervous, but calmed some of his jitters by doing what he did best—going out on the ice and flattening anyone on the other team who got in his way. The first day, it was defenseman Terry Carkner and winger Claude Boivin. The next day, it was veteran right wing Kevin Dineen, whose father was the Flyers' coach.

"He has a little bit of a mean streak in him," Bill Dineen said with a smile. When told that Eric said he was holding back—after all, these were his teammates, not actual opponents, that he was pounding into the boards—Dineen smiled. "He said he's holding back?" the coach said. "I think Eric's going to be given a lot of room on the ice. He's so big. I don't think there will be too many guys who'll want to get too close to him."

But Eric could do more than hit, as he showed in his first game before the home fans. He had a goal, an assist, and a lot of physical play in the Flyers' 4-3 exhibition victory over Quebec. "It's always a great honor to score your first goal at home," he said, "and getting it against Quebec certainly felt good."

Still, Farwell tried to keep Flyers fans from getting too excited. Eric was, after all, a rookie joining a last-place team. "Although we're bringing in a potential superstar and a player I think will change the game," he said, "he's only 19. We don't expect him to come in here and play by himself."

During the off-season, the NHL had negotiated a new television deal with ESPN that got the league much greater exposure. It also gave Eric a national TV stage for his NHL debut on October 6, 1992, when the Flyers opened their season against the defending Stanley Cup champion Pittsburgh Penguins.

Eric didn't disappoint, scoring a spectacular unassisted goal 31 seconds into the third period to spark the Flyers to a 3-3 tie. Three nights later, he got his first game-winning goal, stealing the puck from New Jersey defenseman Scott Niedermeyer at the Flyers' blue line and beating Devils goalie Chris Terreri on a breakaway with less than five minutes left to snap a 4-4 tie as the Flyers won 6-4.

"He has to be patient and strike like a shark," said teammate Brian Benning.

Flyer fans also needed patience. Though Eric had 8 goals and 15 points in his first 13 games, the Flyers went 3-7-3. They were winless in seven games until Eric gave them a shot in the arm in a game against St. Louis on November 7.

Eric took exception to the way Blues defenseman Lee Norwood was roughing up Flyers defenseman Gord Hynes and squared off with Norwood. The St. Louis veteran managed to tie up Eric briefly, but the Flyers' rookie worked his right arm out of the jersey and won the fight.

A sold-out Spectrum roared its approval as the Flyers rallied from a 2-1 deficit for a 4-2 victory. But Eric refused to take credit for having done anything extraordinary. "You do what you can to get things going," he said. "I wouldn't say it was a real jump-start. But it was something that had to be done."

By now, Eric was playing with Mark Recchi on right wing and Brent Fedyk on the left side. The line was dubbed "The Crazy Eights" because of their uniform numbers—Fedyk wore number 18 and Recchi had number 8 to go along with Eric's 88. The Crazy Eights nearly drove the New York Islanders nutty, combining for 13 points in an 8-5 victory on November 12 and adding 12 more in a 7-2 victory over Ottawa three nights later. Three of the seven goals belonged to Eric, who recorded his first National Hockey League hat trick.

But the good times didn't last long. One week after the hat trick, Eric suffered his first serious NHL injury. He went to check Buffalo defenseman Petr Svoboda, but an instant before the hit, Recchi shoved Svoboda to the ice along the boards. Eric tumbled over both players and caught his left knee on Svoboda's helmet. He went down and couldn't get up.

The diagnosis was a sprained ligament—quite a blow to a team that had won five straight games and was starting to feel good about itself.

"He's going to get hurt once in a while," said Farwell. "He plays wide open and runs into people. I don't think you can change the package."

Lindros skates hard at the 1993 World championships.

When he got hurt, Eric had 28 points in 21 games, tops among NHL rookies, and the Flyers had improved to 8-9-4 to get into playoff contention. The doctors originally told Eric that he would only miss about two weeks of action, but the injury was worse than originally feared. He wound up missing 27 days. The Flyers went 2-7-0 in that span before Eric got back on the ice and set up Recchi's winning goal in a 3-1 victory over Chicago on December 19.

Eight nights later, Eric scored on one of the NHL's rarest plays, a penalty shot. He beat Washington goaltender Don Beaupre with 18 seconds left in regulation time to give the Flyers a 5-5 tie. Eric may have rushed back onto the ice too soon, however. Two nights later, he aggravated the same knee he had hurt in November during the pregame skate at Los Angeles, costing him two more games. The same problem flared up two weeks later, forcing him to miss more playing time.

Although Eric was producing well over a point a game, the injuries had cost him any chance of winning the Calder Trophy, given to the NHL's Rookie of the Year—not with Winnipeg's Teemu Selanne on the way to a record 76-goal season. They also cost the Flyers a chance at the playoffs.

But Bobby Clarke, now the Flyers senior vice president and the driving force behind the club's Stanley Cup triumphs in 1974 and 1975, wasn't discouraged. "He has a chance to be the best player who ever played," said Clarke, a member of the Hockey Hall of Fame. "People are physically afraid of him, and they should be. He's got that fire inside him that allows him to smack someone if it's needed."

In all, Eric missed 12 games before coming back with a bang, scoring twice on February 9 in a 7-1 victory over Ottawa. He struggled through the next few games before his confidence really returned, scoring three goals and adding four assists in a three-game span. He also resumed flattening any opponent who got in his way.

"A lot has to do with confidence," he said. "Sometimes when you break through checks, you feel stronger. Then you're not wearing down; you're getting to the guy and hitting him. That sort of refills the tanks."

While Eric kept putting up points, the Flyers continued to struggle. He broke the club record for goals by a rookie, scoring his 35th goal of the season on March 24, in a 5-4 win over the Rangers at New York, a game in which he recorded his second hat trick. The victory was part of a season-ending eight-game winning streak that gave the Flyers their best finish since 1987-88. Eric finished the season with 41 goals and 75 points in just 61 games. The most telling numbers were the 23 games he missed—and the Flyers' 7-14-2 record while he wasn't in the lineup. Not even a sensational showing for Canada at the World Hockey Championships, where he had 11 goals and 17 points in eight games, could alter the fact that Eric couldn't carry the Flyers all by himself.

The Flyers knew it, too.

INSULTS AND
INJURIES

For the first time in three years, Eric was not hockey's hottest topic during the summer months. Instead, he was able to enjoy his accomplishments as a rookie and look forward to his second season.

"I'm not going to say I was satisfied with my season and I'm not going to say I was disappointed," he said of his initial NHL season. "I look at the stats and see that if I had stayed healthy [instead of missing 23 games with knee injuries], I was on pace to score well over 100 points."

As for the demands and expectations he could expect in his second season, Eric said "we deserve more pressure this year. It makes the game more enjoyable. Let's turn up the heat a little."

Farwell wasted little time making changes with the team. The biggest was to replace Bill Dineen

Lindros celebrates an assist as teammate Mark Recchi has just scored. Early in the 1993 season, Lindros led the league in scoring, but injuries would hamper his output.

as coach. Dineen's fatherly style may have made him popular with the players, but his fate was probably decided when the Flyers missed the playoffs for the fourth straight season. A key addition was rookie right wing Mikael Renberg. The 21-year-old Swede showed a surprising scoring touch in training camp, and it wasn't long before he would wind up as Eric's right wing.

Before the season, the Flyers named Kevin Dineen as their captain, the first time since Rick Tocchet was traded in February 1992 that the club had officially had a captain. There was much talk that Eric should receive that honor, but team management felt that, at age 20, he already had enough demands on his time. He was named as one of the team's alternate captains, an honor in itself for a player just starting his second NHL season.

Eric's rise to the NHL's elite was confirmed in October 1993 when *The Hockey News*, the unofficial bible of the game, rated him as the NHL's top power forward for his combination of skill and strength. "He's scary," Toronto defenseman Todd Gill said. "You don't go into the corners first with him. You go in together so that he can't take a run at you."

Eric was the only player on *The Hockey News'* list who was not a wing. This only served to point out his combination of speed and power, since centers don't usually do a lot of work along the boards. But Eric, even in only his second season, was no ordinary center.

"At the start of the game, there's no one at the reins in terms of the control and flow of the game," he said. "You can get some control by getting some hits and being forceful."

Both Eric and the Flyers got off to a hot start. He had goals in three straight games as Philadel-

Lindros lies on the ice after being injured in a collision with a Buffalo Sabre.

phia opened with a 5-1-0 spurt. The Flyers were counting on Eric for a strong start, and he took the expectation in stride.

"I'm not putting a lot of pressure on myself," he said. "I'm here to have some success and some fun. The only way you have fun is when you win. You put a certain amount of pressure on yourself to win, but I'm not going to live like so many people expect me to live. It's just not going to work. But in a lot of respects, my 'life skills' seem to have improved. Everything seems to be even. Nothing is out of whack."

Farwell noticed the improvement in Eric, both on the ice and in dealing with the pressure of being "The Next One." Writers had given him that nickname because he was expected to be the

NHL's next great player, much as Gretzky had been known for years as "The Great One."

"He's very focused in his approach," the general manager said. "The shape he came to camp in and the way he's handled every request have been great."

Both Eric and the Flyers stayed hot through the first month of the season. Eric had 14 goals and 25 points after the team's first 16 games, in which the Flyers went 11-5-0 to take over first place in the Atlantic Division. Just when everything seemed to be going perfectly, Lindros suffered another injury.

In the first period of a game against New Jersey on November 11, Eric was bumped by Devils forward Bill Guerin in the Flyers' zone. He skated for several seconds before being knocked down, then he struggled off the ice. Almost a year to the day after Eric had torn a ligament in his left knee, he suffered a partial tear of the same ligament in his right knee.

"It doesn't feel as bad as the injury last year," he said. "I couldn't even get up under my own strength then."

Eric went back to Toronto to have the knee examined by another doctor, but while he was home, he developed a urinary tract infection and had to take antibiotics for three weeks to clear up the problem. That meant that he couldn't work out, and it delayed his recovery from the knee injury.

Just as they had the year before, the Flyers struggled without their young star in the lineup. They were 5-8-1 in the 14 games he missed before returning on December 16. Eric's timing was off and his energy level appeared low in the first few games after his return.

With the club in a 1-7-1 slide, Coach Terry Simpson moved Recchi off the line with Eric and Renberg and put Dineen in his place. The move sparked the Flyers, as Eric scored his first goal in well over a month on December 27 in a 2-0 win over Buffalo, and then celebrated New Year's Eve by scoring the game-winning goal in a 4-3 victory over Boston.

The struggles continued. The Flyers lost games at Dallas and Tampa Bay to finish the first half of the season just one game over .500 after starting out 12-2-0. Both Eric and the Flyers were struggling to find the winning form they had enjoyed before his injury.

They showed signs of improving as Eric's hat trick helped the Flyers beat St. Louis 8-3 on January 19, and Simpson said that Eric was starting to look like his old self. "He's been emotionally ready to play, and physically, he feels a lot more confident," Simpson said. "He's taking charge, and that's what we're looking for."

Philadelphia fans were watching Eric grow up. He was accepting his role as a team leader and becoming more good-natured about dealing with the hordes of writers and other media that surrounded him after every game. "I remember when I had a really bad game as a rookie and I stormed out of the locker room," he said. "Bob Clarke caught me in the runway and told me to get back into the locker room. He told me that if I had a bad game, I still had to go back in there and answer questions."

The team struggled again after the All-Star break in late January, losing their first six games after the midseason contest in New York and going 1-8-1 in a 10-game stretch that dropped them under .500 and into fifth place in the tough

Atlantic Division. Eric's scoring touch was returning—he had 35 goals and 71 points in just 49 games—but the Flyers were struggling defensively. Simpson kept changing the left wing who would play with Eric and Renberg, trying to get more offense when the second-year star wasn't on the ice.

Eric wasn't the only Flyer to be injured, either. With Dineen and All-Star defenseman Garry Galley sidelined in early March, Eric, who had turned 21 on February 28, stepped into a leadership role. He had a goal and five assists in an 8-2 rout of the Ottawa Senators on March 10 and left the Senators singing his praises.

"He has everything," said Senators defenseman Darren Rumble. "He's big, he's fast, and he's one of the most skilled players in the league. Whatever type of game it is, he can adjust."

In 55 games, Eric had already piled up 39 goals and 45 assists for 84 points—nine more points than he had in 61 games as a rookie. "There are nights when he's just impossible to stop," said Washington coach Jim Schoenfeld after Eric bulled past All-Star defenseman Al Iafrate to score a goal and set up another in a crucial 3-3 tie at Washington. "He just gets up a head of steam and . . . whoosh."

While Eric, Renberg, and players like Recchi and Rod Brind'Amour piled up points, the Flyers' defense and goaltending were struggling. With two weeks left in the season, Philadelphia was four points behind both Washington and the brand-new Florida Panthers, who were in their first NHL season, in a three-way race for the last two playoff berths. Losses to the New York Rangers and Calgary put the Flyers in jeopardy of missing the playoffs for the fifth straight season, for now they also trailed the New York Islanders, who were mounting a late playoff charge.

Eric had a highlight-film goal in a 6-5 win at Hartford on April 2 but was sidelined again two nights later when he was crunched into the boards by Washington defenseman Igor Ulanov, spraining his right shoulder. He had to miss a 3-3 tie at Florida on April 7 and could only sit and watch three nights later as a 4-3 loss to Boston officially ended their playoff hopes.

Eric wound up with 41 goals and 97 points in only 65 games, winning the Bobby Clarke Trophy as the Flyers' Most Valuable Player for the second straight season. Renberg profited from Eric's passing skills, finishing first in the league among rookies with 38 goals and 82 points.

Personally, Eric had had a good season. Between injuries and his team's failure to make the playoffs, however, he still had a lot to prove.

MVP

The failure to make the playoffs cost Coach Simpson his job. When Eric came back in the fall, he would be playing under his third coach in three NHL seasons. This time, though, Farwell was gone, too. Clarke, the former Flyer hero who had proved his skills as a general manager in Minnesota and Florida, was brought back as president and general manager.

The Flyers made it clear that expectations were high. New coach Terry Murray, an old friend of Clarke's, walked into the locker room on the second day of training camp and announced that Eric would be the team's new captain. "I was a little bit surprised," Eric said. "I didn't think it was going to happen right away."

Eric was among the youngest captains in NHL history—and because he had usually played with older players, it was the first time that one of his

Brother Brett Lindros was a top pick by the New York Islanders in the 1994 draft. After suffering several concussions, he had to retire without having reached his full potential.

Lindros had a great season in 1995 and won two most valuable player awards.

teams had given him the "C" on a full-time basis.

"He's our best player, and we expect him to lead by example," said Clarke, himself a former Flyer captain. "There's no reason for him not to be captain of this club. At this point, it's the right move. Eric possesses the leadership qualities and abilities that it takes to be captain."

With his status on the team at a new level, and the goaltending situation improved by a deal that brought back Ron Hextall from the Islanders, Eric was ready to lead the Flyers toward the playoff berth that had eluded them. But then the NHL's labor problems intervened.

The regular season was scheduled to start October 1. But the prospect of playing a second straight season without a labor agreement was more than the owners were prepared to accept. Instead, they announced that the players would be locked out. No games, no fans, no goals.

Instead of hitting opponents, Eric wound up hitting the books. He had taken college courses before signing with the Flyers, and he now took advantage of the unscheduled time off by taking courses at the University of Western Ontario.

"I really found this enjoyable," Eric said. "I'm not just talking about the learning. I had no idea of how much you get out of going to college. Just something like college spirit is impressive. Our football team won [the Canadian national championship], and you could feel the excitement."

It looked like Eric might get to spend the whole year at school. The stalemate dragged on through the fall, past Christmas, and into 1995. With the time for saving the season running out, the owners and players finally settled their differences in mid-January and a 48-game season was scheduled.

The Flyers got off to an awful start. Eric battled a case of the flu that forced him to miss one game and weakened him for the next two. Eric had 11 points in his first 10 games, but the Flyers were just 3-7-1 and it was obvious that something had to be done. The question wasn't whether a trade would be made, but who would be dealt.

The answer was Recchi, the team's number one scorer over the past two seasons. On February 9, he was sent to Montreal for defenseman Eric Desjardins and forwards John LeClair and Gilbert Dionne.

LeClair, a huge left wing with a big shot, was regarded as a disappointment in Montreal. Although he had scored two overtime goals in the finals to help the Canadiens beat Los Angeles for the Stanley Cup in 1993, he never put up the scoring totals that had been expected of him. Dionne, the brother of Hall of Famer Marcel Dionne, had never followed up on a half-season in which he broke the 20-goal mark.

"We had holes that had to be filled," said Clarke, "and one-for-one trades weren't going to do it."

Desjardins helped settle down the Flyers' defense, but LeClair proved to be the missing piece of the puzzle. Murray put him at left wing with Lindros and Renberg. But Eric was still struggling. He went six games without a goal, the longest drought of his career. It was his first prolonged slump in the NHL. "Everybody goes through it," he said. "I'll be getting out of it soon."

Eric was true to his word. He broke his six-game drought by scoring three times in a 6-6 tie with Quebec on February 23. All of a sudden, Eric and his linemates were scoring—and the Flyers were rolling.

The Flyers went 11-3-2 in their first 16 games after the trade, with Eric, LeClair, and Renberg leading the attack. They became known as the "Legion of Doom," both for their scoring ability and their size. LeClair and Renberg each weighed about 220 pounds, about 10 less than Eric—but a lot more than most of the forwards and defensemen trying to stop them. No one could remember a three-man unit that combined that much size, speed, and talent.

Having big linemates took some of the physical load off Eric, for which he was grateful. "It has saved a lot of my career," he said. "The abuse I went through my first year—you can't do that for 15 years and have solid years. Having two guys forechecking along the boards is great. I don't have to be so physical. I haven't been running around so much, and I've been able to improve the other aspects of my game."

In their first 16 games, the Legion of Doom scored 36 goals and totaled 76 points as the Flyers moved to the top of the Atlantic Division. Now, instead of writing about Eric's injuries and struggles, reporters were speculating that he had

become the best player in the NHL. Ottawa coach Rick Bowness said that Lindros was the player he would pick if he could choose one player around whom to build a franchise. Even Messier, Lindros's idol, called Eric "the prototype player of the '90s," adding, "there's going to be a time when a player like that wins the Stanley Cup."

On April 20, the Flyers officially ended the longest playoff drought in the NHL by beating the Islanders 2-1 to clinch their first postseason berth since 1989. Eric felt the team was capable of a lot more. "We can really contend for the Stanley Cup," he said. "I really think we have a good enough team. If everyone plays as well as he can, I don't see why we can't do it."

Eric's showing was vindication for owner Ed Snider, who had given up so much to get him three years earlier. "He's the most exciting play-

The Flyers shake the hands of the Sabres after Philadelphia ousted Buffalo from the playoffs.

er in the NHL right now," Snider said. "It's especially satisfying because I think this was the gutsiest deal ever made in sports. We said Eric was going to be the best player, and we were right."

The Flyers wrapped up the division title with a week to go in the season, and Eric appeared to be headed for the scoring title when he was the victim of a freak accident. In the Flyers' next-to-last game on April 30, Eric's slap shot hit Rangers defenseman Jeff Beukeboom, then bounced back into his eye. Lindros collapsed to the ice and was taken to the locker room with a five-stitch cut and a bruised left eye. He sat out the rest of that game and all of the Flyers' season finale against the Islanders, finishing the abbreviated campaign with 70 points. The eye injury more than likely cost him the scoring title, because Jagr caught him on the season's final night. Both finished with 70 points, but Jagr won the Art Ross Trophy because he had 32 goals to Eric's 29.

Eric had to sit out the Flyers' first two playoff games against Buffalo, but he came back to lead the Flyers to a five-game blitz of the Sabres. He was even better in the second round against the Rangers, rampaging through New York's defense and neutralizing Messier, the heart and soul of the defending Stanley Cup champs. The Flyers won the first two games at the Spectrum in overtime, then polished off the Rangers with two wins in New York.

The Flyers then had to face the New Jersey Devils in the Eastern Conference finals, with a trip to the Stanley Cup finals on the line. The Devils knew they had to shut down Lindros and his line in order to win, and made sure that checking forward Claude Lemieux and their largest defense pairing, Scott Stevens and Ken Daneyko, were on the ice as much as possible when the Legion of Doom was out there.

The strategy worked. New Jersey limited Lindros and his linemates to just five goals in six games. The Devils won the first two games in Philadelphia, but the Flyers pulled even with a pair of victories in New Jersey, with Eric scoring in overtime to win Game 3.

The series went back to Philadelphia all even, and Game 5 appeared headed for overtime with the score tied 2-2 in the final minute. Lemieux shocked the Spectrum crowd when he blasted a 50-foot slap shot past Hextall with 45 seconds left in regulation time, giving New Jersey a 3-2 victory. Two nights later, the Devils ended the Flyers' season with a 4-2 victory. The Devils ended up winning the Stanley Cup, defeating the Detroit Red Wings.

Getting so close to the Cup and not winning was a disappointment. Even winning the Hart Trophy as the NHL's Most Valuable Player and the Lester Pearson Trophy as MVP as voted by his fellow players was not enough to erase the sting.

"It's a long grind, a true war," Eric said of the playoffs. "It does wear on you," he added about his frustration at the tight checking he received from New Jersey. "You go out don't touch the puck for a shift and feel like you haven't done anything. It eats you up."

Clarke said, "He's 22, so he's going to learn," Clarke said. "It's his first playoff experience, so he's going to learn—and so are the rest of our young players."

The only consoling factor for Eric and his teammates was that, as the third-youngest team in the NHL, their best days were still ahead.

MOST POPULAR PLAYER

Eric started the 1995-96 season right where he had left off. He was honored as the NHL's Player of the Month for October for scoring a league-leading 21 points, 10 goals, and 11 assists, as the Flyers raced out to a 7-1-3 start. He had points in all 11 games and led the league with a plus-14 rating, meaning that when he was on the ice the Flyers scored 14 more non-power-play goals than their opponents.

Eric kept scoring, but the Flyers struggled for the first half of the season, unable to find enough offense when the Legion of Doom wasn't on the ice. He recorded his 300th NHL point on December 15 by setting up LeClair's 100th career goal in a 6-1 victory over Dallas on January 15, and he reached the All-Star break in mid-January with 59 points in 38 games. The Flyers, however, were third in the powerful Atlantic Division, trailing both the New York Rangers and the upstart Florida Panthers.

Lindros is checked during a 1996 playoff game against the Tampa Bay Lightning.

Lindros got to charge down ice with Wayne Gretzky at the 1996 World Cup.

Though Eric still liked to hit hard, he'd learned that he had to pick his spots better to be of the most value to his team. By the second half of the season, he was making a more conscious effort to avoid unnecessary scraps with less-talented opposing players, who hoped to lure him into taking dumb penalties. In a February 3 game at St. Louis, he repeatedly turned away from Blues tough guy Tony Twist, who was trying to bait him into a fight that could have robbed him of five minutes of valuable ice time. Rather than fighting, Eric retaliated with his stick, scoring his first hat trick of the season in the Flyers' 7-3 victory.

"Better him than someone who can skate," Eric joked after his eighth three-goal game in less than four full NHL seasons.

Though Eric had developed a longer fuse on his temper than he had had as a 19-year-old, he was still willing to fight—as Buffalo's Bob Boughner found out in the Flyers' next game. After being poked by the Sabres' defenseman once too often, Eric dropped the gloves for the first time in two months—and Murray felt that despite the penalty time, his captain did the right thing. "That's one of those situations in which he's challenged four or five times, the guy pushes on his chest and it ends up where he has to do something," said Murray. "He feels he has to do it and he did the right thing."

"I was just trying to spark something," said Eric. It didn't work, though—the Flyers lost 2-1.

By mid-February, the Flyers were 10 points behind the Rangers. With Renberg hurt and a number of other players injured, Murray briefly switched Eric to right wing on a line with LeClair and newcomer Dan Quinn. But no matter where he played, Eric kept scoring. He celebrated his 23rd birthday with goals number 40 and 41, as the Flyers skated to a 4-4 tie in Dallas on February 28. He was now seventh in the scoring race with 87 points, and the Flyers were beginning to creep up in the standings.

By mid-March, they were still third but trailed the first-place Rangers by just three points. More importantly, the Flyers had moved to fill the void left by Renberg's injury by acquiring veteran Dale Hawerchuk from St. Louis, who earlier in the season had reached the 500-goal mark. Hawerchuk had five points in his first three games and the Flyers went 10-1-0 in their first 11 games after the deal.

The race for first place was now a two-team affair. The Flyers passed the Rangers on April 2 with an easy 6-2 victory over the Islanders, then staked their claim to the top spot by knocking off the Rangers 4-1 at the Spectrum two nights later. Lindros was a key to the big win over the Rangers, setting a career high with his 45th and 46th career goals. Thanks to a pile of goals by LeClair, he had earlier passed the 100-point mark for the first time.

Even though Eric missed two games with an injured calf, the Flyers' victory run continued. It came to a head in the final days of the season. The Flyers celebrated their last regular-season game in the Spectrum with a 3-2 victory over Montreal that clinched the Atlantic Division title, and they wrapped up the Eastern Conference championship on the final day of the season by beating Tampa Bay 3-1. Eric finished sixth in the NHL in scoring with 47 goals and 68 assists for 115 points, despite missing nine games due to injury. He was third in the NHL in points per game at 1.58, trailing only Pittsburgh stars Mario Lemieux and Jagr.

Eric was a target for Tampa Bay in the opening round of the playoffs. The Lightning felt that they could bother the Flyers' star by belting him at every opportunity. Eric sustained a bruised kneecap when he was hit from behind by Igor Ulanov in Game 2, but got even with Ulanov and the rest of the Lightning in Game 5.

With the series tied 2-2, Lindros took command early in the fifth game, checking Ulanov into the boards so hard that his helmet came off. Less than 30 seconds later, "Captain Crunch" flattened another pesky Tampa Bay defenseman, Michel Petit, with a board-rattling hit that left Petit laying on the ice.

Goalie Ron Hextall felt Eric's physical play set the tone for the Flyers' 4-1 victory. "Eric sparked it," he said. "They weren't very happy with the hits Eric put on them. They seemed to be running around after that."

The Flyers polished off Tampa Bay in Game 6, ending the series with a 6-1 victory at the ThunderDome. That sent them into the Eastern Conference semifinals against Florida, a third-year team making its first playoff appearance.

But the Panthers had a core of veterans, including goaltender John Vanbiesbrouck, who frustrated the Flyers throughout the series. Eric had the winning goals in Games 2 and 3 as the Flyers took a 2-1 lead in the series. After Florida pulled even with a 4-3 overtime win in Game 4, Eric gave the Flyers a 1-0 lead midway through Game 5. But it wasn't enough, as the Panthers tied the game in the third period and won it on Mike Hough's goal in the second overtime. Two nights later, on May 14, the Panthers ended Philadelphia's season with a 4-1 victory.

Although he put up the best scoring totals of his career, Eric had to settle for a second-team All-Star berth behind Pittsburgh's Mario Lemieux, whose amazing comeback included a scoring title. But he was number one in another area. *The Hockey News* reported that he was voted as the NHL's most popular player in a survey of its readers. After some of the bad press that he had endured earlier in his career, Eric was delighted that fans had come to appreciate his skills on the ice.

"I had no idea," he said when told of the results. "It certainly makes me feel good. After everything that's gone on and the way things turned out, this is something special. I'm lucky."

Eric's summer was shorter than usual because he was picked to play for Canada in the first-ever World Cup, the successor to the Canada Cup, which he had helped his country win in 1991. This time, though, Eric was counted on to be a star, not just a contributor.

With Canada struggling offensively, Eric was seeing more and more of the opposition's top checkers. That, combined with what turned out to be a painful groin injury, limited him offensively. His biggest goal came in the tournament final, when he scored late in the second period to pull Canada even with the United States at 1-1. The Canadians took a 2-1 lead in the third period, but the Americans scored four late goals to win the game and the tournament.

In 1997, Lindros played in only 52 games due to injuries, but he was healthy when the playoffs started. He was brilliant as the Flyers ousted Buffalo in the second round. In the next series, against the New York Rangers, Lindros clearly got the better of his childhood hero, Mark Messier, and the Flyers advanced to face the Red Wings in the Stanley Cup finals.

Detroit swept Lindros and crew, and Eric did not score a goal until the last seconds of the final game. He said he's never been more disappointed in his life.

At age 24, Eric Lindros has already enjoyed the biggest individual highs the NHL has to offer—except one. As long as he can remain healthy, chances are he'll get another chance at winning the Cup soon.

STATISTICS

ERIC LINDROS

Regular Season

Season	Team	League	GP	G	A	PTS	PM
1988-89	Can. National	.....	2	1	0	1	0
1989-90	Det. Compuware	USHL	14	23	29	52	123
	Can. National	.....	3	1	0	1	4
	Oshawa	OHL	25	17	19	36	61
1990-91	Oshawa	OHL	57	71	78	149	189
1991-92	Oshawa	OHL	13	9	22	31	54
	Can. National	.....	24	19	16	35	34
	Can. Olympic	.....	8	5	6	11	6
1992-93	Philadelphia	NHL	61	41	34	75	147
1993-94	Philadelphia	NHL	65	44	53	97	103
1994-95	Philadelphia	NHL	46	29	41	70	60
1995-96	Philadelphia	NHL	73	47	68	115	163
1996-97	Philadelphia	NHL	52	32	47	79	136
1997-98	Philadelphia	NHL	63	30	41	71	134
1998-99	Philadelphia	NHL	71	40	53	93	120
NHL Totals			431	263	337	600	863

Playoffs

Season	Team	League	GP	G	A	PTS	PM
1989-90	Oshawa	OHL	17	18	18	36	76
1990-91	Oshawa	OHL	16	18	20	38	93
1994-95	Philadelphia	NHL	12	4	11	15	18
1995-96	Philadelphia	NHL	12	6	6	12	43
1996-97	Philadelphia	NHL	19	12	14	26	40
1997-98	Philadelphia	NHL	5	1	2	3	17
NHL Totals			48	23	33	56	118

GP	games played	PTS	points
G	goals	PM	penalty minutes
A	assists		

ERIC LINDROS
A CHRONOLOGY

1973 Born on February 23 in London, Ontario.

1989 After the Ontario Hockey League changes its rule banning trades of first-round draft picks, Lindros is dealt from Sault Ste. Marie to Oshawa for three players, two draft picks, and $80,000.

1991 Is named the OHL's Player of the Year after recording 149 points in only 157 games; Eric is picked number one overall in the NHL draft by the Quebec Nordiques; Eric is a member of the gold medal winning Canadian team, which beats the United States for the Canada Cup title; he then returns to Oshawa after declining to sign with Quebec.

1992 Scores the shoot-out goal that gives Canada a quarterfinal victory over Germany at the Winter Olympics and Canada goes on to win the silver medal; Eric is traded by the Quebec Nordiques and both the Philadelphia Flyers and New York Rangers claim they've acquired him... Lindros joins the Flyers in exchange for five players, two draft picks, future compensation and $15 million. He signs with the Flyers during the summer.

1993 Named to the NHL's All Rookie team after scoring 41 goals and 75 points.

1994 Plays in the NHL All-Star Game for the first time; after scoring 44 goals and 97 points, is named as winner of the Bobby Clarke Trophy as Flyers MVP.

1995 The Flyers acquire left wing John LeClair from Montreal and team him with Lindros and Mikael Renberg, forming the "Legion of Doom" line; an eye injury forces Lindros to miss the final game of the season and Jaromir Jagr ties Lindros for the NHL scoring title; Lindros wins the Hart Trophy as the NHL's Most Valuable Player and the Lester Pearson Award as the NHL's MVP as voted by the players and is named a First Team All-Star.

1996 Enjoys his first 100-point season and is named a Second Team All-Star; despite his game-tying goal in the tournament finale, Canada loses to the United States in the finals of the World Cup.

1997 Leads team in points, assists, and penalty minutes during playoffs.

1998 Scores 500th goal in February; misses 18 games late in season with a concussion.

1999 Suffers a collapsed right lung and misses final seven games of the season; signs a one-year, $8.5 million contract with the Flyers.

SUGGESTIONS FOR FURTHER READING

National Hockey League Draft Guide, 1991. New York: National Hockey League.

National Hockey League Official Guide and Record Book, 1993, 1994, 1995, 1996, 1997. New York: National Hockey League.

The Hockey News Yearbooks: 1991, 1992, 1993, 1994, 1995, 1996, 1997. Toronto: Transcontinental Sports Publications.

Hockey Digest Yearbooks, 1991, 1992, 1993. Evanston, IL: Century Sports Publications.

Philadelphia Flyers Media Guides, 1993, 1994, 1995, 1996.

Woolf, Alexander, "Winning by Losing." *Sports Illustrated,* August 30, 1993.

ABOUT THE AUTHOR

John Kreiser has covered the National Hockey League for more than two decades for newspapers, wire services, radio, and magazines. He spent more than 15 years as a staff writer at *The Associated Press*, where he handled a variety of assignments, including four seasons on the NHL beat. A contributing writer for *Hockey Digest* and *Rinkside* magazines, he is also the coauthor of *The New York Rangers: Broadway's Longest Running Hit*, the first complete history of the Rangers.

A graduate of Regis High School and Fordham University in New York City, John, his wife, Helen, and their five children live on Long Island.

INDEX